ch

MW01707960

For Sonia,

Blessings on your Journey.
May all health and healing
be yours

Chris

Further Up and Further In

Further Up and Further In

Chris Marks

LYRICALMYRICAL

Author's Photograph: mae hah lum
Cover painting: Sarah Beaudin
Cover design: Sarah Beaudin
Editor: Luciano Iacobelli
Typography: bellina works

Library and Archives Canada Cataloguing in Publication

Marks, Chris
Further up and further in / Chris Marks.

Poems.
ISBN 978-1-897275-74-0

I. Title.

PS8626.A75415F87 2013 C811'.6 C2013-900924-8

Published by LyricalMyrical Press
www.lyricalmyricalpress.com

Printed in Canada

This book is dedicated to the memory of my parents,
Audrey and Gerry Marks, and is just another way of saying
thanks to them for setting the whole thing in motion,
kick-starting my journey through time.

CONTENTS

A LITTLE RAMBLING POEM ON ZEN AND THE ART OF: PAMELA ANDERSON LEE: A REAPPRAISAL (HER CHANGING ROLE WITHIN THE TRADITIONS)

I could have sworn I had the hinges oiled
and the windows cleaned just the other day
but it's dawned on me anyways there's still something wrong
with my doors of perception they open and close
                                                                                    open and close
exactly as they're supposed to like it says in the manuals
but you'd be amazed at the stuff that gets through

for instance

just the other evening it's eleven thirty p.m.
I'm about to close down the factory for the night
I've given the employees a couple of days off
my senses are about to punch the time clock
on their way out the gates

I've every intention of spending the weekend in a coma
(a coma or radiant trance)
my protestant consciousness has saved up quite a few sick days
and is looking forward to languishing guilt-free in bed
no more worldly aspirations no more desires and regrets
just languishing unawares in bed
                                                            while who knows maybe
the lord God and his angels from somewhere beyond
call it the cloud of unknowing take over the show
and refresh me refresh me like rain

and something inside me will blossom
blossom like eliot's multifoliate rose

but no,
it seems a couple of the labourers have signed on for overtime
I can't for the life of me get them out of the place
I'm restless as hell in my oval ego office
barking orders at the recalcitrant staff

"a memo! another damn memo!
listen youse two! If one more of these memos
from the outside world
crosses my desk
                                        before monday morning
you're fired! got it! history! the pair of you!
now get out! scram!"

but it's no good so I pick up the remote
and start switching from channel to channel

I notice that the canadian girl pamela anderson lee
is on one of the talk shows brought to us so kindly
by our neighbours to the south she's making the rounds
with her much-reduced boobs does she or doesn't she
still have a career now that THEY'RE mere shadows
of their famous former opulent selves

which is all well and good, but there's more

it turns out pamela she and her art
have been greatly maligned I had no idea
she was the sort of girl who would go out of her way
to stay and there's no other way to put it ABREAST
of the latest developments in literature and thought
she's taking this opportunity to make her final
non-verbal statement
not the finger of desire pointing at the moon
of her bosom and ass but the bosom and ass themselves

or maybe it's me.

(remember the trouble I was telling you about
re my doors of perception)
but maybe it's not

because as I'm watching this program lovely pamela lee
commences to embark upon a stunningly original occult performance
she actually begins to deconstruct herself
right before my eyes
you'll be happy to hear
she hasn't for a moment forgotten
any of the lessons she learned in the exercise
of her previous craft
but she's taken the whole thing to a completely new level
it's like a buddhist or existential striptease

one by one she removes the clothes of her flesh
a nose an ear an arm a leg
it all comes off and vanishes
into wherever it vanishes POP
goes one body part and POP goes another
there's a clever
and extremely satisfying
metaphysical moment
when her right arm disappears
and the hand that's attached
doesn't go with it
but remains there for a while
suspended in space
the fingers twitching in rhythmic succession
almost as though they were keeping time to the music
of this profound and sublime mystical erasure

as the host cuts away to the final commercial
all that remains of statuesque pamela
is a kneecap an ankle and earlobe alas
that same kneecap ankle and earlobe alas

that I myself included with so many men
have nibbled on in dreams
                                        both waking and asleep

however, to conclude:

whether or not in this latest incarnation
as queen maya the mother and high priestess of illusion
she deemed it necessary to make for the benefit of all beings
and the psychological health of the great groaning universe
exactly this kind of daring ontological demonstration
I really don't know,
but the facts remain now and forever the same
the physical constituents of the woman
formerly known as pamela anderson lee
have been absorbed into something
like matter's unconscious

therefore

if I have a headache tomorrow
or a new nervous tic
I'll know thank goodness where to place the blame
It may take centuries to fully digest
this latest unveiled phenomenon
the new pamela factor in spiritual life

though maybe what I should do is call
the renovators in and have them re-design
those damn doors of perception once and for all

LOCATION LOCATION LOCATION

I fired the garden variety
garrulously good-natured oaf of a real estate agent
with whom I had serious differences of opinion
about the inherent value of properties
both tangible and non of course
and replaced him with a curious fellow named huxley
who admittedly was almost blind
but seemed to know his way about town.
he spoke with sober eloquence of a perennial philosophy
and directed me to an old part of town just recently
under re-construction.
when God moved into the neighbourhood, everything improved
and no-one ran away. the smoke
from the factory next door all but disappeared. there was even
talk of closing the factory for good   this factory of the
unregenerate self which belched out 24/7
the noxious fumes of the usual suspects the 7
deadly sins all former at one point in time
very dear acquaintances of mine.
you wouldn't believe the changes, huxley exclaimed.
you can see the sky again and the mountains in the distance
not to mention the houses across the street.
notice how everyone's planting a garden.
there's a sacred fire at night and hymns
to the unmanifest. the air again's for breathing.
people have started talking to one another again
the cop on the beat smiles and whistles a tune
and the neighbourhood children join in
the crime rate has miraculously plummeted
the man with a knife in his hand and the crazed look
of diabolical exultation on his face is forever
sheathing his knife
and the divine life within you has been spared.
if you're looking to lay down some durable roots
you can't do better than this.
Come and join me

UPON RECEIVING MY FIRST ISSUE OF ARC MAGAZINE

yes, I like poetry.

I also like beer and hockey and golf.
and women's bodies.
mornings and watching my breath.
my mother who struggles at 92 to hang onto her mind .
and total I mean total not so much
as a word a peep poetic or otherwise
silence,

though far be it from me to disparage to make light of
anyone's efforts in the expressive arts
it's of paramount importance that we have our say
in this curious fashion industry of thought,
show what we've got what we're made of
strut our stuff
especially to wax a little linguistic
when is seemingly isn't
or in our sorry case as in all others
has an extremely short shelf life
we need to console ourselves with the caresses of language
the subtle and probing fingers of sounds
which touch us over and over again
where it counts
in the long days and nights of the absence

yes I like poetry

CELLBLOCK 17

freedom you call it
but really all you're doing
is looking out the window of your cell and dreaming
punctuating your bios, your endless fantasy life
by scratching learned (yes always learned)
graffiti on the walls
for the amusement and edification of the next prisoner
and that grand misunderstanding you call God
the seductions of self life
the liquid curves of her body
your hunger and thirst
a smile and an apple
the promise of the bliss you gave up
only so you could seek it again
in this strange dimension of time
you were about to enter
have landed you none other than here.
which isn't of course where you were
nor where you want to be
on the other side of ecstasy
a fast flowing river that divides the world
into plurality and unequal parts
madness and distraction just outside the window
beyond the yard for exercise
your somewhat limited social sphere
where all that you know of the ghetto and jungle
is put to good use

the truth is it's hard work
freedom costs exactly everything
no more and no less
and it won't be recaptured (an unfortunate word)
in a day

but if you whittle humbly away
with that knife that was smuggled in
on a visit by an old friend who knows
something just might be done yet

SUNDAY MORNING

staring through the blinds
at the vast expanse
of the moose factory sky
egg smeared in octopus shape on the window
black poison of ennui spilling from tentacles
spreading like lingering night through my slow waking brain
the clouds are unanimous
the earth has no quarrel with rain
I envy the universe its agreement and non-resistance

trees are asleep all around us
a few vehicles go by
on these aboriginal roads
I wonder should I or shouldn't I
bother with church and the litany of words
as the buddhists say is it useful
anything more than a diversion
the lord's supper a symbol
of what should always be the case,
but isn't

then busy with rapprochement
moving about the apartment
forcing myself to engage
cello music a river I fall into holding my breath
seeking the treasure of the eternal self
the radiant plenitude of that
which just will not be spoken
down among the seaweed and crabs

I'm not really here
but I've picked up a trick or two along the way
I'm friendly to the day
in all of its guises
to lampshades and cupboards I serve tea with a smile
and gracious conversation

important people approve of my style
I'm encouraged to make a more durable statement
I tell them I feel like a child on a swing
swinging back and forth between being and non-being
stretching my toes in the air
I speak in my best purgatorial voice
I've picked up a trick or two along the way
I can wisecrack if I choose
with time and delusion
I can speak with conviction
of what I don't really know
where is the zen exclamation point
among the myriad of question marks
I'm not really here
I don't know where I'm hiding
why it's taking so long
am I just around the corner
or am I already here
and I simply don't know it
is this confused vigilance and deferral my career

....

I paint in borrowed and semi-enlightened language
the picture of a tombstone with the words of an epitaph
I await my arrival engraved on its face

A NON-SHANNON KIND OF FULFILLMENT

first bach
then shostakovich
now bartok

not shannon in toronto
with all the subtle pleasured nuances
of her radiant black skin

– whose bright splash of beauty
on the canvas of my soul
stirs such desire

the labyrinth of whose nakedness
I must enter like theseus
chasing down the minotaur
trailing a thread of to do's and don'ts
oughts and responsibilities
just to make damn sure
I can find my way out again

– no, not shannon in toronto
but music in moose factory
is my very special friend today.
I sit quietly
and listen to all it has to tell me
of joy and suffering madness and death
and is it my imagination
or do I really hear
the ever leaping note
of the divine as well
(breaking the roiling surface
dolphin sportive in the sea)

a tree grows
the reality tree grows
in the soil of my being
I sit in its shade
and catch the fruits
of a non-shannon kind of fulfillment
as they fall through the air
fall from the sound branches twisting and turning
in the nothing of god

A POET'S MEMORY AND PROGRESS

I lay in the ten thousand infants' brain
of the singsong of the sun and was happy

but then I opened my eyes
(which is when when began
and when exactly is when
anyways)
awoke to this suffering
this pulsed animal circumscription
unbuddhaed by biology and kind of tough to avoid
craving
old nobodaddy's dharma and higher mathematics
half-assed being and awareness checkerboarded
with dukkha
                    darkness and pain
something's not right here
surely they gots the wrong man
I watch the clock on the wall
and pick at the scabs of mortality
for employment and something
like heart's ease

MYSTIC AMBITION (or WHO DO YOU THINK YOU ARE)

a bit of foolishness at church on sunday
briefly I reproved God for not making me a spiritual master
the adept of my generation a da avabhasa
who doesn't mess up   transmitting
body and soul bathing love in luminescent siddhi
spiritwaves of blessing to each and every member
of the congregation   who better than me
for the job
    or humbler because
I can do humble quite well   just a trumpet
of prophecy to unawakened earth
the realization of shelley's mystic ambition

but emerging from a reverie
of the miraculous and dizzying
dark spaces within   of which I suspect
I am the exclusive and sole proprietor,
I notice the priest's good looking wife
with a twinge of envy and regret
shake hands with a man I occasionally dislike
pick up the tune where I left it
hum the first monotonous notes
of the music of self-love
before noticing the statue of christ
on the cross at the front of the church

DAYS AFTER

yesterday it was rivers of bird delirium
winds of bewilderment raging through my skull
the visible becoming invisible growing claws and a beak
stones on the bank that spoke in a prophet's voice of blood
and blood appeared
ecstasies of water and light
being crucified and reborn in the stalks of flowers
the scales of fish
agonies and birth pangs of mountains
hunger and thirst for the infinite
hunger and thirst for no thing
the painted wind of consciousness
awareness opening
stars of paradox burning so brightly
thought in its pedagogy
erasing itself in spools on the slate of night
the word spoken unspoken
then spoken again
thin air of abstraction
breath of annihilation
the hidden world
unhidden in phantasm and enigma
I run my fingers and voice over the body of the ineffable
dark venuses rising on waves of the unknown
waves of the unknowable
black holes of the nameless
concupiscence and failure the unlimited limited
I don't forget for a moment that I am dying
and like keats half in love with
I grow tired of this hide and seek game with presence and language

EVENING OF SEPTEMBER 22, 2010

read a few chapters of the pickwick papers,
an old favourite,
hoping that the genius of dickens
at his comically sunniest and most large-hearted
would lift me out of the well
out of the to use the familiar image from bunyan
slough of despond I'd fallen heavily into.
no such luck.
so difficult it is for the wayfaring spirit in this life
to stay just one step ahead.
indulged like an unwise parent my complication and conceit.
as bertrand russell said of nietzsche
trying desperately to cheer myself up.
watched a little television.
tried to get worked up about a preseason hockey game
and the pretty girl on channel 8 who reminded me
of a young woman in toronto whose time and attentions
I pay for.
my eros crucified on the cross
of my own bad habits and life choices.
uncertain what I want is more or less consciousness.
felt sorry for myself.
meditation. then bed.

MARTYR

it's six of one
half a dozen of the other
(which of course would make twelve
a somewhat significant number
in this type of thing)
but it makes no difference in the long run.
no doubt some of us know what we're doing
and some of us don't.
whether we're really out for blood and agony
or simply honing our skills
                                                  our bowmanship
engaging in what seems at the time
like nothing more than a little innocent target practice
the effect remains the same.
and even though there might be
a crack of thunder here
a flash of lightning there
(a disapproving growl if you like
from the cosmos)
we're moved only to take careful aim once again,
and strictly speaking we do not miss the mark.
our arrows puncture and pierce
the holy and redeemed flesh of silence
like st. sebastian tied to the stake
of our incomprehension and fear.

six of one
half a dozen of the other

FOR A FRIEND WRITING A BOOK

these words both fear and welcome
their own demise
spilled like an avalanche of cold white horror
on the solitary skier
gazing at the moon and checking his pulse
they aren't going anywhere and are already there
(they write themselves while writing themselves
after they write themselves again)
erasing themselves
                                        leaving no tracks
cancelling all appointments
settling for a desk job
diving into extinction but always
coming up for air
for a breather
not completely enveloped
a last will and testament
apocalyptic love song to death
wearing medusa make-up
in front of invisible mirrors
never quite prepared to surrender the sound
of their own orotund mystery
where do we go from here

to fields of justice and humanity
spread out like a map in the sun
or picnic blankets for the gods
the rounded blue wonder of a robin's egg
the slippery freedom of a glide across lakes
verbing   being
but never verbed been enlightened dead or to come
a hand nailed to a cross
a hand scribing circles in the air
mouthing the carcass of the world

spitting out like bullets
machine gun fire   promiscuous   indiscriminate
murder in the flesh
cold blood
                    slitting the throat
of that tyrant abstraction

and carrying on
                         carrying on

OR DO I HAVE TO FIGHT MY OWN BATTLES

in a whisper I speak it
I daren't go out again today
they lie in wait for me as usual
outside the door of my soul
affecting a casual air
whistling an innocent tune
the bullies and toughs in the employ
of my enemy
hair slicked back like in the 50s
t-shirt sleeves rolled up past their shoulders
cigarettes dangling from their mouths
fear and guilt etched on their knuckles
ready to pounce at the first opportunity
at the first step outside
my besieged residence
I ask myself again and again
those protection racket boys
those bright energies and angels
the ones with the suits and the violin cases
the bodyguards and guarantors of happiness
what do I pay them for
isn't the way it works is
I forks over an agreed upon sum
in the recognized currency of the spirit
the dollar bills and coins of prayer
credit cards and cheques of charity
and it's hey diddle diddle
the cat and the fiddle
by which I mean to say I'm free
I should be free
but I'm anything but I'm not
so what in God's name do I pay them for

THE AENEID: BOOK 3

as you're being booed and hissed off the stage
by that demonic crew which periodically
sets up camp in your head
when you don't get the words right
when your delivery is all wrong
when the small personal self
rises up like a monster from myth
and seems to be all that this world is about,

it's important to keep a few things in mind

you will get away from this latest scrape
this latest scrape with the forces of evil.
the ragings of your self and other destructive ego
a blind polyphemus dripping blood from his eye
roaring and stumbling out of the mountainous thickets
down to the water where the sweat of your flesh has drawn him
a bloody feast for his ravenous maw on his mind
can and will be eluded.

your destiny is not here, just as it will not be
with any of a number of didos in carthage.
yes there are sibylline rumours of another season in hell
but at the moment these are nothing but rumours.
the important thing is to keep going your work
is not yet completed. the divine
is your mother and wise nobility your father.
and this is your inheritance.
not death in the towering flames of an earlier
misguided contest with the angry energies of life.
(or any of the other
deaths of the spirit which surround you)

your life is a pilgrimage
and the heart an epic hero
on its way to found the empire of heaven
in the prophesied earth of your soul

BLOOD IN THE URINE

my bright shining tongue
upon which a virgillian seer on cowboy horseback
sings the eternal glories of the imagination
and lassoes the sun the gods and the totality of history
with a golden rope of language
and tosses them luminous at your feet
before winking and waving a hat (preternaturally white)
laughing and riding into the beautiful horizon
of slowly fading light (slowly fading light)
is all but swallowed up today
by the voracious black maw of death.

it's amazing what a little blood in the urine will do.

TO A YOUNG POET

you cut with the sharp knife of your mind
a hole in the fabric of let's call it
reality for now
stuff it like a christmas bird
colloquially trussed and punctuated to a "t"
with as much articulate dressing as you can muster
and there's always champagne for the occasion
a communal celebration of nobody's
quite sure what
dinner with friends and other strangers
the cutlery absurd
and smiling at a joke
you know you were born to get
I am not afraid I am not afraid
you murmur
                    into her ear
the void you have so carefully crafted
staring you in the face
to face

MIRROR

my friend asks me
what does emptiness charged with energy
look like
and I refer him to this poem

one by one
this poem takes all of its thoughts off
and piles them neatly in a corner
like a fastidious suicide

is it a little bit like holding the breath
of your mind

perhaps
what do you see

A CRITICAL RESPONSE

you and I my friend are as one.
we like what we like, and don't like the rest.
I'm exactly like you my brother.
I support the advancement of learning.
I fly the flag of the american dream on my lawn.
I'm full of the world and capable
of all the necessary and correct self-assertions.
I aspire against beauty in my down time
plot over drinks to subvert the transcendent order.

I too have worked all day
at a job that is less than satisfying.
taxes are too high.
the environment's a mess.
my sex life troubles me no end.
there are wars all over the globe.
and time whispers about me behind my back.
(I walk always with a pebble in my shoe)

I enter the room and don't like what I see
the poem on the floor in a meditative posture
cross-legged and breathing in breathing out
hanging on every word of something I can't hear
I loathe and despise its eternal detachment
the way it smiles and pays me no heed
its serene expression its non-partisanship
its aristocratic approach to prayer
the way it organizes itself around a nullity
its unhurried heart and apophasis
the cat and mouse game it plays with ideas
its eschewing of the modern idiom
its old fashioned presumption of meaning and significance
the way it struggles to rhyme with the infinite
the way it holds out stubbornly for a blessing

its commentary that reads like a love letter to God
its metre that turns into air
the perfect circle it nearly describes

when the poem is in this kind of mood
given over to the asana of silence
at rest in this insulting inwardness
in danger of losing itself in losing itself
(and thereby finding itself it claims)

and all else fails even noise wonderful
noise chaos of sound pandemonium
the percussion of pots and pans and screams
screams that you make when a hungry bear
wanders into your camp –

don't panic

its flesh will taste good in our mouths

GO I

have you read this book
he asked me
this is a wonderful book
holding up a dog-eared copy of john irving's
a prayer for owen meany
sitting cross-legged on the sidewalk
in the practice of the indigent
shivering in the toronto cold
just a week before christmas
outside the always bigger is better
self-proclaimed
world's biggest bookstore
huge holiday smile on his face

yes. yes I have
I told him enthusiastically
this down on his luck jesus
streetcorner jesus capitalism's orphan
for whom they haven't quite finished
building the cross

and I dropped a few coins in his cup

STORM POEM

gusting up to 90 kilometres and roaring
the wind means business outside
almost snow in september in moose factory
leaves from the colourful head of autumn
thrown madly desperately aside
what became of cold mountain's natural opus
the season convulsively grieves
in lacerated precipitation against the window
its own passing once again without point
the flux and the flow continue
the earth cycle persists in behaviours
which always fail to bring about
the hoped for the sought after result
finally ready for the psychiatrist's couch
buddhists assert there is no permanent self
but still something inside me is happy
when taking another day off
I lie on the chesterfield reading
a tale of two cities again
my love and admiration for dickens in my 50s
unchanged from when I was 23

YEAR'S END

a little grumpy a little asocial
and almost always short of sleep
I think it's safe to say
I'm not always the best of hosts
but tonight I throw open the door
to memory
to old loves and absences
wandering like vagrants
from one street to the next
indigent
begging on streetcorners
lost in the limbo of past time
waiting to be reclaimed
to be set free
pinching themselves for assurance
staring at themselves in mirrors
storefront reflections
just a little too proud
a little too wary
to check into a shelter for the night
choosing the raw air the urban outdoors
in even the most extreme of weather
standing in line at soup kitchens
or sharing a bottle of mouthwash around a back alley fire
sleeping on sidewalks and park benches
ravaged   rent   torn asunder
pleading for mercy
whipping themselves with cords of shame
forget-me-knots
and speaking with no-one
but talking out loud
expostulating bravely
arguing with fate and destiny
scoring points against invisible opponents

hurting   insane
but refusing medication and treatment
simply not buying it
not believing what they're told
not believing what they're not told
circumambulating their hopes and fears
their dereliction
like devotees their spiritual master
muttering nonsensical mantras
asparagus sea serpent cold cuts banister and the queen

I throw open the door and let them in
try to give them succour for at least one night
hug each of them in turn
bless and am blessed
discuss the weather and spiritual warfare
corruption in high places
gunshots
and all that I've become
raise a glass to celebrate their return
to greet with a kiss the new year
the old adam made new again
made new again in the birth of a child
wisdom's acknowledgement in a manger
of our indigenous divinity
but I don't think they get it
at the end of the evening they refuse to depart
they cling to me like a savior
hold onto me like a cross
and I'm stuck with my ethereal friends
my memories time's martyrs hungry ghosts
who care little if they've outlived their welcome
or if the present and the future are calling

SON OF MAN

christ
who is you who is me
comes from the undivided
now   and now   and now
but something's in the way,
though I can ape with startling mimesis
the movements and sounds of the words
which would cleverly mime and suggest
otherwise   (words like the proverbial
damned, bereft of all freedom and soul.)
I can take photographs of language
with the most technologically advanced of equipment
and display them on the walls
of any new age exhibit in town
but this absurdity no longer appeals.
sometimes I meditate
and sometimes I devise the most exquisite of tortures
for all those who have gotten on the wrong side
of my resentment.
and sometimes I pray.
sometimes I go into the backyard
and mixing the earth of friend with the earth of foe
water with cruel determination blake's poison tree.
I'd rather recline on a touristy beach
beneath the sun of love and stillness
a cool drink at my side a novel in my hands
than endure these storms of division in my head
but it seems I can't afford at the moment a vacation.
there's too much work to be done.
something urgently real to be born.

DESIRE OF CORRUPTION

there are no surprises here.
it's all very simple.
don't be alarmed by rumours of my peculiar metaphysic.
I know why I'm here.
and I know what I want.
I want your youth and your beauty.
I want to hold them in my arms and grow strong.

free from the casket of the dead and the mundane
I want to sink my teeth into your neck
and fill my dry veins with beauty's sweetest seeming ambrosia.
for years I have been married
to the most divine of philosophies
but adapting with skill and ingenuity
my favourite meditative posture
in order to get a better view of your charms
today I contemplate not the sublimest of unions
with the source and fountain of all being
but only your buttocks and maybe your smile
and all of the lesser fidelities.

I want to lie beside you at night and take notes
and carefully convert them into gold and strawberries
open a booth at the local farmer's market
and sell the fruit of my labour and passion
to an unsuspecting public
which so readily mistakes that which passes
for that which is incorruptible and lasts.

my case, undeniably, is a curious one.
I know the score only too well.
I willfully ignore my soul
for the sake of the moment
and traffic only in perishable things.

I have lost all interest in the still points of heaven
the non-history of the unmoved mover
but invest all of my time and attention
in the supple motion of your body
as it walks across a bar
and the lascivious smile you casually toss my way
the noblesse oblige of the young and the pretty
the prasad of the cold and the lecherous for hire

boyfriend of the dying
lover of the mutable
affianced once again to all that is temporary
I throw away years of practice
to lay my exploding head on the bosom of the ephemeral.
with you in the room
I even find death amusing.
I ride my middle aged fever
like a wild horse
through the summer flames
of a city in heat

IT AIN'T GOOD, AND SOME ARE ARTISTS

unlike God
we talk too much
and speak the world into non-being
seventh day of creation blues notwithstanding
tell ourselves that it is good very good
i's have been dotted t's have been crossed
we haven't wasted our time after all
spinning the honeyed web of language
from out the centre of our disconnect
filling up the scary white spaces
with the colourful palette of our desire
fiction of course is our métier
fencing the nothing in with words
singing into sentences and verse paragraphs well punctuated
whole volumes of discourse and entertainment
along the carefully marked rhythms of a chanting voice
really not having much of a clue
what we're talking about
but talking like crazy
writing like mad
of the making of books
there is no end
holding a mirror up to non-nature
the vacuum we've learned to comfortably inhabit
the seductions of the life fantastic
reality is simply too much work
reaching out our arms to embrace the ghost of a lover
we have conjured in reflections of our own forlorn selves
on any surface that will have us
any eyes that will behold us
who exist only in our troubled
we like to tell ourselves triumphant
and bearing down all before it, imagination

ABSURDITY

a friend of mine a real aesthete
and intellectual through and through

even on vacation next to the sea
sticks to his cultural guns

(a serious man a serious man
echo the inrolling waves at our feet)

not caring a fig for the apparent inconvenience
he lugs down to the shore every day

meticulously sets up in the sand
a beautiful framed rendering of the ocean

so he can continue he proudly says
his contemplation of the glories of nature

A MEMBER OF THE AUDIENCE

both hands grasping for dear life
the thin cord of the balloon of language
legs dangling preposterously in the air
he ascends (or thinks he does) like jesus
in a transfigured body
or elijah in a chariot of fire
into the realms of impossible light
green coins of ambition transmuted
into the largesse of heaven on the page
wild swans of the imagination
chasing down the bread crumbs of emptiness
truth as transparent
as delicate and intricate as a rhinoceros's egg
or a drunken butterfly's wing
jabberwockies of wisdom
twisted scrolls of obscurity and subjective arcana
lit up like love from within
silence espoused and worn loudly like a hat
doffed graciously to the rest of us
those of us less fortunate less blessed than THE POET
who is with us thank god today
but it's anybody's guess
for how much longer.

hurry up please it's time

time to forget your worry and marriages
this incarnation which never feels quite right
your troubled offspring and culture out of control
the cosmic jokes you still don't get
the fear of death like an unanswered question
you keep coming back to
our poet after all hosanna in the highest
our poet is here

here and now
holy and sublime
magisterial amongst the affinities

so we watch and applaud (but never enough)
the performance
one hand clapping

MISTAKE

not good not good.

I chase the joyful little spirit
quickbounding around me and barking
incessantly
arguing in a tailwagging language all its own
on behalf of the day
and the strong affirmations of light
against my estrangement and stubborn
refusal to play
my moods shot through with death and apology
away

PRAYER

amazing from strictly a detached point of view
(and we both know how long that will last)
to watch the mind transmogrify into a whip
and flagellate itself with promiscuous abandon
surely this if anything
is a kind of penance which will bear no fruit
the ropes the handcuffs the shiny black leather and mask
so you've got just the right amount of impersonality
and mystery
the hint the suggestion that you're a voyeur watching
the working out of something like cosmic justice
the morning after and its eschatologies
at the end of a prolonged and bewildering courtship and trial
the passing of a kafka-like judgement on your soul
which is executed here in the chambers of love
it isn't you know always about the money
the great whore gracing you with a personal and unsolicited
appearance
the bright red lipstick like an accusation
naked then and down on all fours
because at this point in the proceedings
you've chosen your side
humbly submitting to the commands of mistress
not sure how you feel about your erection
from such orgies of sado-masochism in truth and in the spirit
I pray Lord to be delivered

THE TEARS I CRY TODAY

the tears I cry today
are for the children I do not have
the unborn ones
who loiter in the vestibule
of pure potentiality
awaiting their call
awaiting their summons
my daughter thel
who shivers in the cold bardo of winter
without so much as a blanket of compassion to cover her
awaiting the fire and purpose of my love
which I cruelly withhold
nonchalantly cutting the deck
for another game of cards with death

and my son my son
delinquent in cities and towns of the infinite
genius of streetcorners and violence
sheltering at night in dreams
beneath gates of the wisdommother
longing for the fertile land of the heart

I cry for these today
and my tears form a pool
where I swim for refreshment
and stare at myself
the wind of a voice from the forest
ripples the surface of the water
tears on the page of the poem I am writing
the crossword puzzle I labour to solve

ADVICE TO THE READER

none of us wants to believe
that the lines of a poem
can be like a rope around the neck
of your joy, but still

for the sake of your equilibrium
and the high wire act we call living
best not linger here too long
no longer than is necessary
staring in bewilderment
at the words on the page
this page a river
where the body of a six year old
floats
                                        incomprehensible
to say the least
the workings of justice move on
move on

THE BEST LAID PLANS

just outside this poem
which always turns out
much different than I plan it
the devil's henchmen
a pair of them
each with a rap sheet
centuries long
a couple of low lifes
time's mercenaries
death and nihilism for hire
lean against the side
of the uncertain small building
(the original blueprint
was for a temple)
which this poem is constructing,
chainsmoking cigarillos
taking pulls from a bottle of cheap whiskey
cussing and spitting on the naïve flowers
the roses and chrysanthemums the poem laboured
with so much effort to grow
timing the spit to the imprecation
the imprecation to the spit
guffawing at one another's awkward
forays into humour
slangwhanging insults
leafing through the pages
of glossy porn magazines
the money shots of snuff flics
genocidal cum
a photo album of war crimes
traffic in small children
the sleaze of history
starting to salivate at the mouth
a noticeable bulge in the pants

grinning and touching themselves there
the process gathering momentum
increasing excitement
moving grimly   inexorably
towards the payoff
ecstasies of evil and oblivion
(yes there's a word for it
that which has a kind of existence
intelligence and sentience
for that which has not)
where is your almighty God now
they sneer
                    glaring
through the broken window of language
I try to hide myself
and all that I care about
behind

NONPLUSSED

I thought it would be easier this way.
I'd always be on top of things, always
on top of my game.
I've chosen with care my style and discourse
my conquistador's stallion and dress.
I marshal armies of words in the night
assemble mercenaries of grammar to fight
a u.n. sanctioned war against all that is mysterious and unspoken.
I reflexively assume the old-fashioned patriarchal
missionary position of the grand rhetorical gesture.
I believe in God, I believe in God.

no bliss it's true
no virtuosic glide over the ten thousand things
(hawk-winged howl of beauty
skimming the egregious surface
of the lakes of this world)
no push from the spirit
up the steep sisyphean hills of samsara
– no birth from above.

but no terror either
no descent into hell no return
match with the devil
the headspinninglindablairedswirling
sucked under upwards and inwards
downwards and around turn and turn about
hell of personal intimate beelzebubbling confusion.

we all make sacrifices, and at this point in my life
I choose my battles judiciously.

I like to tell myself that I reason well
have sat at the feet of many a logical argument
many a syllogism.
I practice an acrobatics of thought
perform a high wire act of ratiocination
both with and without a net.
when asked I can summon up
opinions on the news
on elections in both this country and abroad
with presidential persuasiveness and authority.
sports of all sorts continue to interest me.
I have important views on feminine beauty and hygiene
real estate and the olympic games.

but alas
it's with no small measure of embarassment
and chagrin
that I sadly confess
that just the other day
when a local aboriginal up here in moose factory
asked me politely for my opinion on the wind
I had nothing to say

what to do what to do

A NAÏVE QUESTION FOR A FRIEND

because the complex skepticism of the age
is yours, and extinction most of the time
seems like nothing to write home about
you tie the frayed strands of your thought
into grim secretive knots of no-meaning.
call this willfully complicated subjectivity
its occasional intersection with rumours
of history and personal narrative poetic.
feel anything but liberated in the moment.
life really is a headache at times.
you've read all of the necessary authors
culled judiciously from the syllabus of gloom.
and despair you do very well. no-one would ever
deny it. but tell me

can you move your feet to the exuberant steps
of an uncryptic dance in the heart?

ABSENCE

and among the hierarchies of angels and gods
man's absence is vigorously debated
a voice raised in prayer
is missing in action they say
the bright beam of attention nowhere in sight
the transcendent white light of devotion where is it
starbursts of energy and illumination
earth on its knees
freedom of obedience majestic choral gratitude
the gift given and the gift received
the knight of the cross is lonely
what a lamentable state of affairs is this
a few of the impatient extremists
(by some called heavenly nihilists)
even going so far as to pronounce
in stentorian tones unequivocally
the final nail in the coffin
MAN IS DEAD

CHOICES

given the choice between the scratching the head
but still patting oneself on the back miraculously
impossibly   paradoxically   ,
just for making the prodigious effort etceterly
apophatically
esoteric intellectual sophistication of say
blanchot in translation
who tells us I believe among other things
that we can never linguistically speaking actually die
and the goodhearted but sorely put upon christian
woman across the street from me in moose factory
whose sister died a few years ago by her own hand
I choose the goodhearted christian woman every time
who's learning like me a little more each day
to follow the divine directive
be still and know that I am God

IN MEMORIAM

here's hoping there's no shortage of jokes
or something like whiskey in heaven
ambrosia I suspect is a taste easily acquired
in the pubs and lounges of the resurrection
all blessings then upon the memory
like the faint whisper of the wind in the trees
of the earth being you so charmingly were
and still are,
though somewhat different now I believe
surprised and surrendered seachanged in God
both more and less of yourself
desmond maxwell
scholar wit mentor and friend

NOT THE DAY OF REST I LOOKED FORWARD TO

afflictive emotions jostling for position in the town square
hurling insults and stones before setting aflame
a perplexed image of myself in effigy
a crowd of lonelinesses and desires at war with one another
megalomania and shames and sadnesses
boredoms and embarrassments both sympathizers and collaborators
I can see where all this is headed
rioters run amok smashing windows overturning cars and buses
and the priggish underground leader a deranged ayatollah
tucked away nicely
the superego hidden from view
in some other city some other land
no way of tracing his involvement
but still pulling the strings calling the shots
of this morally strident and flagellant revolution
he will have more than his pound of flesh
did you or did you not
take advantage of yourself in the night
what kind of sorry little self-loving and self-loathing
fool of a hedonist are you
a myriad of voices point fingers
another cop car is tipped over
there's a surge towards the government offices
a man is knifed and a woman screams
like quasimodo I seek sanctuary in the church
struggling to shelter my soul in its pristine state
from all the forces of a hypertrophied conscience
which would make of me and my cause
if only I could remember it a martyr
damnit damnit damnit
there's just too much going on too many of me
to fit into
to do justice to what could have been the refreshment
of solitude today

JOB WELL DONE (SCENE FROM THE LIFE INTROSPECTIVE)

it was a bit of a surprise really... not what you'd expect... in one of the on the surface anyways... quieter and more civilized... neighbourhoods in town... the dome it was called... short maybe... I really don't know... for domicile... or something else... but like I said... it was not what you'd expect... either those of us in the peculiar business we're in... or anyone else... citizens of this thriving... and God-fearing metropolis... but nature... human nature... go figure... one thing's for sure though... the whole thing had gone on long enough... the ruckus had continued... unabated... all day and all night... the call came in... at about 1:30 in the morning... and we responded... my partner and I... in the blink of an eye... we tore through the streets... siren blaring... lights flashing... and arrived at the scene...of the complaint... in next to no time... the party... the neighbours told us... as we got out of the car... had started early... about mid-afternoon... music and singing and laughter... intoxicated harmonies if you will... communions of ecstasy... no separation at all... just like you read about in the spiritual manuals... the air redolent with incense... and divinity... but things as they often do... took a turn for the worse... harsh words and anger... chaos ensued... the monkeys in the brain... shaking the bars of their cage... spitting and throwing words... like feces... at the onlooking ego... who recoiled in fear... in a chair in the corner... revolted by the shit... which sticks to its oversensitive skin... egads!... what a torment!... my life has been!... quoth the ego... anyways... to the echo... of our screeching tires... we arrived... as I've already said... at the scene of the crime... and were greeted... from within the old brownstone... with a cacophony of curses... a pandemonium of profanity... fuck off you bastards!... go fuck yourselves and your mother!... and little girls!... in hell!...and such-like abuse... hatefully sexual... and demonic in nature... my partner... a man of few words... and a veteran… on both the theological… and existential beat… was all for storming the bastille… going in guns ablazing… but I settled him down… a last resort I remonstrated… so we heaved with our shoulders… exercised our boots… burst open the portal… highly trained professionals… enforcers of law… is what we are… what we do… in a matter of moments… I say with as little pride as is possible… we had subdued our quarry… apprehended the pneumatic perps…slapped on the cuffs… and frogmarched the noisy brawling thoughts… those dark energies of the mind… out the door… and over the manicured lawn… to the squad car that was waiting… at the side of the curb… around which a small crowd… had gathered.

WISHES

for example

having read the introduction I humbly submit
for divine adjudication
that there's something important to be learned
from kierkegaard's sickness unto death
so in all fairness let's face it
this is really touch wood an unpropitious moment
for my death
the dialectic of finitude and infinitude
requires in my case significantly more time
as it inches and spins
towards the final resolution
that tongue ripped out and cast aside

terminus

the timing's horribly off life lessons incomplete
my love affair with the beautiful
dark feminine curves of language
surely has a few miles to go

and what's more this canadian winter I'm really enjoying
the novel snow by orhan pamuk so do you think
we could forestall like put off my departure
from this curiously happy and unhappy world
that yes I know I've become too comfortable in
just a wee bit longer

etc.

MORNING (THE CASE OF)

but then something I record it here one hand on the bible
something happened. I write it
as dispassionately as I can
a witness an unlikely instrument of truth
singing with a shaky voice in holy fear.
morning arose from its slumbers and was given
what it was convinced it no longer deserved
– a fresh start, a clean slate.
                                        in the blink of an eye
the earth had been taken to the cleaners
and returned in time for breakfast.
history began all over again.
air moved freely   uncontested
in and out of lungs.
he was scrooge on christmas day.
morning hardly knew how to receive such a gift.
he had never been much of a praying man
but this turn of events called for special measures.
he opened the window of his apartment and hollered
a full-throated hallelujah at the neighbours.
and as chance, or providence, would have it
there was a church around the corner.
morning hastily threw on some clothes
covered the shame which he no longer felt
and bicycled to the service
a huge thank you like an eagle flying out of his mouth

FROM THERE TO HERE (THE SHORT OF IT)

I travelled through the slow, heart-sounded
deep rhythm of love
to the oh so nervous
                                        lands and country
of dysfunctional prophetic urgency
daily to quote myself
checking the temperature of the eternal man
wondering if and when he'd ever
pick up his pallet and walk
now I
          love never forgotten
in the threatening winter light
skate across the surface of reality
on silvery blades of mantras and silence

A SORT OF EPISTLE: FROM ONE FAILED MUSICIAN TO ANOTHER

7 kids were gunned down at a prayer meeting
in texas yesterday
and I'm still angry with my friend

the invisible choirmaster touched me on the lips
and asked me to sing
a not unreasonable request given that
there's some kind of choral symphony in progress
and occasionally just occasionally it seems as though
I get it I really get it I hear it
the kingdom that's spread out before us
in sun and moon and clouds and trees
deep earth bass notes too

but on this particular occasion
(and I confess there have been many)
after preening myself in the mirror
                    of my own complicated self-absorption
wheels within wheels within wheels
                              of my curious existence
and after applying the necessary preparatory spray
to my vocal chords
when I opened the deep throat of my conduct
for all to see   for all to hear
only a horde of ungainly raucous
                         belligerent frogs jumped out
there was murder and cruelty and deceit
and numberless introverted betrayals in my voice

but the choirmaster let me sing on
the choirmaster lets us sing on
make your action a song he urges

a song you'd be proud to sing
well to put it mildly it hasn't happened yet
we barge into the party dressed
to the nines
and the music we make is not at all harmonious
not at all right or good

our host (praise be) is a forgiving one
a forgiving one again and again and again
(there hasn't been a flood since a bible ago)
but if you think about it seriously for a moment
what on earth are we actually doing
as guests let's face it we're lousy
competitive boorish and ill-mannered at our best
hateful and violent at our worst

at each of your births
you walk into this room
there are violins and cellos guitars and pianos
harpsichords oboes drums and bassoons
and if you look over there there's one helluva voice
gathering dust in the corner

and something or other call it truth that which is
the tao whatever
                                        is just waiting
waiting and waiting and waiting
for us to pick ourselves up by the bootstraps
climb onto the stage and begin

7 kids were gunned down at a prayer meeting
in texas today
and I'm still angry with my friend

do you think maybe it's time
we did something different
with these incredible damn instruments
we've been given

EMMANUEL AND I
(or PLAN FOR THE MORNING)

it's dawned on me lord
that it can't be too healthy
to be stuck forever inside
the small monk's cell
of our tired old definitions
of you
(day in day out
straightjacketed
by our words)
so this morning I've decided
you and I bud
are gonna take a little walk
around the neighbourhood.
while I feed the cat
you chase down
those dusty old sandals of yours
it's time for you to stretch
those celestial legs
a little exercise is good
for both body and soul
but we'll need to be vigilant
on our very best behaviour
(everybody's a critic these days)
as my Italian friend says
you get an accurate glimpse
of a man's (or god's)
true character
simply by observing
how he goes for a walk.
theological tomes
hang in the balance.
an existentially correct step
a stroll with both

ontological heft and decorum
is the perfection of a very human
(and divine) art,
an art in fact equal
to any and all
of the sister arts
involving as it does movement
depth
          silence
and an appreciation of sacred
space.
many of the local gentry
will be walking their dogs
time pushing strollers
yakking on cellphones
another one on the way
the graces playing ball in a park
trees stretch their limbs
in sun salutations
chant happily hello
to the morning
birds argue in branches
about eckhart and you
(don't think you're paranoid
they really are talking about you)
squirrels chatter over nuts
about kierkegaard and love
silences blooming like flowers in gardens.
we might even drop in
on one of the local churches
I suspect it's been a while
since you've been in one of those
your appearance if we're not careful
could create quite a scandal
but we'll keep it as low key as possible
just a pew in the back
quiet responses to the liturgy

no need to upstage the priest.
then back to the streets the world again
all before us
peripatetic matins
breathing in breathing out the mystery
all the way home

PROSELYTIZING

to church this morning I did not go.

but still
                    I was not
if I do say so myself
entirely devoid of christian charity
the greatest it goes without saying
of spiritual virtues.
I spent the hours before dawn
attempting to enlighten
trying to convert my cat
to the one true faith.
something akin I like to think
to st. francis
preaching to that ornery wolf
in the hills around assisi
mend your ways mend your ways
mr. wolf
while there's still time and hope
Christ our savior and love
love sweet gentle love
are the answer.

but alas,
not being a being
quite of the order of st. francis
I fear my efforts were in vain
for after the homily
tig still grinningly hopped onto the ledge
and exchanged hissing insults
with the scruffy feral fellows who gather
outside our window
waiting for me to feed them

and then
(damnation! and lord have mercy!)
the little pagan threw himself
with a bloodthirsty vengeance
against the window
when a winter bird had the audacity
to tantalizingly alight
and flap his wings in a most provocative way
against the glass of said window
which performs the same function
for tig it seems
as television does for the rest of us.

clearly, the saving of souls is not
a facile endeavour.
I must persist in my missionary work.

NO MORE BOGIE GOLF

it troubles an old friend of mine no end
that I'm not at all bothered
by the fact that I'm not
to use language of a different sort
the language of a different discipline
a scratch player when it comes to poetry
ever the noblest of arts he admonishes me.
and of course it's my very own fault.
I'm lazy and undisciplined
always in a hurry
and too religious by far for my own good
always expecting God or the holy spirit it seems
to do the bulk of the heavy lifting

it's true I occasionally hit the thought
fairly well off the tee
even if lacking in the more important yardage
of the joyces and becketts et al
the universally acknowledged masters of this preposterous
game we feel strangely compelled to play (funny
how the irish so often dominate the field)
and much of the time
I do keep the words, or most of them,
on the fairway
with a more or less clear vision
of where I'm going, and how to get there
what club or device to be utilized next
to further the majestic trajectory of truth

well and good.

but there are times there are times o
I freely admit

when I'm all over the place like a madman
up stanza and down simile and assonance
lost in the thick woods and murky waters
of my own metaphors
without so much as a pocket gps
or reliable scorecard to guide me.
and yes I have been known
to throw my writing implements, a pen or two,
while howling dylan thomas like
at the top of my voice
when things don't go the way I wish
especially when flustered and put upon
beyond endurance
sorely tried by a cavernous bunker
the sands say of dullness or predictability

privately
if you catch me on the right day
I'll even own up
to playing not always by the rules
improving or embellishing my lies
(of which there are too many and varied
to tell) all for the sake of the superior
result, and the inevitable clubhouse bragging.
and I'm never I sadly confess
beyond the dastardly and most infamous chicanery
the very epitome of perfidious acts
I refer of course to the most unconscionable
abominable villainy known to man
ie THE FOOT MASHEE
as practiced by blackguards the world over
when stymied by a great and bleeding boulder or tree
paradox or logical conundrum

yes, mea culpa
mea culpa old friend

I do though humbly submit
I almost always enjoy the vistas
the stunning views and intricate cleverness
of the languagescapes (not to mention
the fresh air and company) so I still don't think
I'm completely wasting my time

but still, as the french say
tu as raison
tu as raison

fine tuning you urge fine tuning.
and you're right.
a little more time at the practice range
is just what I need.
one undeniably has to work on one's game.
for the rest of the winter
before the season gets underway
again in earnest
I'll read plato and dante
and your very own brodsky
take as gospel truth and code to live by
yeats's dictum about sedentary toil and the imitation
of great masters

(I might even have the lines inscribed on my ass)

by george I'll step up to the first page
in the spring with a swagger
and an epic invocation in my bag!

TODAY

my french is lousy,
and my voice raised, or rather lifted,
(for I insist upon what I insist
upon) just a little, and with much solemn
effort, into song, almost always
out of key

(stubbornly unnaughted in God)

so for the nonce as they say
even if I dream dreams,
and grasp at visions like straws
to the dying

(grousing rumblings from the belly
of a hungry man)

when I think of st. francis who

picked up a branch from the earth
and laying it on his left arm
he drew in his right hand
another stick like a bow over it
as if on a viol or other instrument
and making fitting gestures
sang with it in french
unto the lord jesus christ

(stigmata flowering
only in imagination
on the soft palms of my words)

the only honest thing for me to do
is bite my lip, hold my tongue
maintain a somewhat less than joyful
even if much happier than before
unmusical silence

THE POET ASKS AN ANNOYING BUT NECESSARY QUESTION

often shiny and feminine and soft to the touch
(variations then on a theme of gollum's precious)
the things of this world are how shall I say
most compelling and curious
        bewitching
        strange
and not without   as the savior says
their own reward

(I speak only of that which I know)

but tell me o self, soul destroying
        man
to whom in the under
statement of the ages
it profiteth so little,
though expert in subterfuge and semantics,
heckler of eternity and eternity's son
(always of course from the best seats in the house
money can buy)

do you never take thought for the morrow,
glad day in its resurrected form,
a golden disc rising
on the mountains and plains
                                        of the strong man
jubilant
in the breast of the one,

the radiant one the cosmos you were meant
to become

GRACIAS

words don't come so easily today
dumb truth walks
through the empty halls of my
voiceways,
overcomes the world
past present and to come
and before I start straining
like a constipated man
to get the correct vocables
in the correct order
all is well because
to say gracias
thank you
as meister eckhart says
just once in your life
is enough so
gracias thank you mister
god

The author wishes to thank the Writers Reserve of the Ontario Arts Council for their generous support.